Welcome to my illustrated world of Christmas Tiny Homes!

Enjoy visiting a charming and captivating world of Christmas Tiny Homes. All the delightful dwellings and quirky residents included in this collection of pen-and-ink illustrations are waiting to be brought to life through color.

Christmas Tiny Homes is the ideal remedy to help shake off that stress and refocus your mind. If it is time for you to take a peaceful and relaxing break, then leave your cares behind with this cozy collection.

 russelljamesart

Published by Hop Skip Jump
PO Box 1324 Buderim Queensland Australia 4556

First published 2022.
Copyright © 2023 R. J. Hampson.

All Rights Reserved. Without limiting the rights under copyright reserved above, no part of this publication may be reproduced, stored in or introduced into a retrieval system, or transmitted, in any form or by any means (electronic, mechanical, photocopying, recording or otherwise), without the prior written permission of both the copyright owner and the above publisher of this book. The only exception is by a reviewer who may share short excerpts in a review.

ISBN: 978-1-922472-21-2

hopskipjump®

Using this book

Find a quiet place away from distractions. Relax and immerse yourself in the process of coloring as you explore the details of each illustration.

This book is best suited to color pencils or markers. Wet mediums should be used sparingly. Slide a card or sheets of paper behind the illustration you are coloring to avoid marker bleed through.

Find fresh coloring pages by signing up to Russell's newsletter. Get free downloadable pages and updates on new books at -

rjhampson.com

FINAL STOP

A SURPRISE DELIVERY

UNDER THE MISTLETOE

LOST REINDEER

AN UNEXPECTED GUEST

A MODERATELY QUIET NIGHT

A MODERATELY QUIET NIGHT

WON'T YOU GUIDE MY SLEIGH TONIGHT?

THE NIGHT BEFORE

CHRISTMAS WREATH

WRONG ADDRESS

NOT EVEN A MOUSE

A CHRISTMAS ODYSSEY

TINY BIRD HOUSE CHRISTMAS TREE

THE LAST PRESENT

VILLAGE FEAST

DECORATING

IT'S ALMOST TIME

IT'S ALMOST TIME

THE OWL AND THE PUSSY CAT

NORTH

SOUTH

EAST

WEST

THREE CRANKY CAMELS

WINDOW SHOPPING

THE HOUSE BY THE LAKE

THE HOUSE BY THE LAKE

Searching for more?

Find new coloring pages by signing up to Russell's newsletter.
Get free downloadable pages, monthly coloring sheets,
and updates on new books at -

rjhampson.com/coloring

Thanks for choosing this coloring book.
If you enjoyed it, please consider leaving a review.
It will help to let more people in on the experience
plus you'd certainly make this illustrator very happy!

Published books in this series

 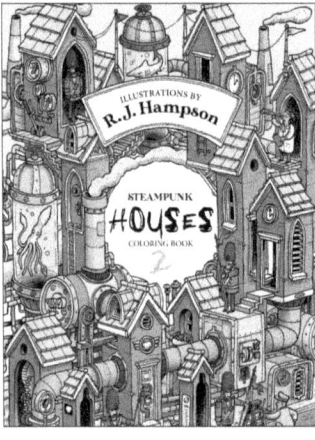  

See flip-throughs and new releases at **rjhampson.com**